Social Security

Social Security

More, Not Less

Robert Eisner

A Century Foundation/Twentieth Century Fund Report

1998 • The Century Foundation Press • New York

The Twentieth Century Fund/Century Foundation sponsors and supervises timely analyses of economic policy, foreign affairs, and domestic political issues. Not-for-profit and nonpartisan, the Fund was founded in 1919 and endowed by Edward A. Filene.

Eisner, Robert.
Social security: more, not less / Robert Eisner.
p. cm.
"A Twentieth Century Fund Report."
Includes index.
ISBN 0-87078-416-1
1. Supplemental security income program--United States.
2. Supplemental security income program--United States--Finance.
3. Social security--United States. 4. Social security--United States--Finance. I. Twentieth Century Fund. II. Title.
HD7125.E36 1998
362.5'82'0973--dc21
97-52354
CIP

Cover design and illustration: Claude Goodwin
Manufactured in the United States of America.

Foreword

Foresight is seldom a routine component of American public policymaking. As in all democracies, the pressure on legislators to deal with immediate problems and the disincentives associated with forcing hard choices on voters combine to validate the old rule of thumb: never take on a problem today that can be left to your successors. Even by the standards of other mature democratic systems, however, recent U.S. experience with "short-termism" is extreme. Experienced political observers tend to assert that it is harder than ever to pursue policies that involve sacrifice now for investment in the future. Statistically, it is apparent that we now spend less on capital in the public sector than in the past. This shortfall obviously will have long-term, negative consequences on future budgets and economic growth.

In this context, the recent explosion of discussions about the prospects of the Social Security system is remarkable. Of course, the program is in many ways a special case—an issue that demands and receives periodic long-term attention from elected officials. The underlying reasons for this exception include the fact that the relevant statute builds in a requirement for seventy-five-year forecasts of the program's economic viability, the shifts in demographic patterns since the program's inception, and the unusually strong public support for continuation of a universal, contributory social insurance program. As a result, there have been numerous adjustments of the program's benefits and revenues over the years.

Since World War II, for example, payroll taxes have been increased twenty times. As recently as 1983, a bipartisan commission developed a set of changes that are today resulting in fairly rapid accumulation of funds in the Social Security Trust Fund. This process will continue for another fifteen to twenty years, when the fund will peak, under certain assumptions, at a total of $1.5 trillion. Then, with the baby boomers retired, the fund, along with future revenues, will be used to meet obligations. After about 2029, assuming average annual economic growth of 1.5 percent for the next century, the combination of the trust fund and payroll taxes would begin to fall short of what would be needed to maintain inflation-adjusted levels of payment.

At some point, under this relatively low-growth scenario, payments would have to be reduced to 75 percent of the current levels (inflation adjusted), a percentage that could be sustained more or less indefinitely. Obviously, under other growth assumptions—for example, continuation of the pattern of modest growth of the past twenty years—Social Security would have quite a different prospect, with all current benefits viable for the foreseeable future.

Given present trends in workforce growth, however, it makes sense to develop strategies to meet the lower growth assumptions. Indeed, there is no shortage of ideas about how to change Social Security. Some proposals, in effect, would scrap the program as we know it, substituting private investment accounts for the present pooled risk and progressive payment system.

A number of these privatization proposals have attracted significant political support. The financial community, in particular, finds this approach attractive. It is not implausible that this is because privatization would create billions of dollars of new revenues for Wall Street and financial firms in general. Some of this money would come out of the additional costs generated by privatization approaches. For example, the overhead cost of the Social Security system is estimated at about 1 percent of contributions. The American Insurance Institute estimates that overhead for insurance companies in the United States is 12 to 14 percent (similar and even higher numbers normally are associated with privatized plans in other countries). Assuming similar overhead for private firms that managed and processed the new private accounts, the potential for additional profits is immense.

On the other hand, there also are many proposals for reform that simply modify the current system in order to meet the changed demographics. The majority of the members of the bipartisan Advisory Council on Social Security, for example, agreed on a set of proposals that would have eliminated somewhat more than half of the forecast gap through relatively modest adjustments to the current program. Others recommended diversifying the investment portfolio of the trust fund, seeking higher returns through riskier instruments like equities, a strategy that, if it worked out as predicted, could go a long way toward closing the gap between benefits and revenues under the 1.5 percent annual economic growth scenario.

A few experts see the present need to address Social Security as an opportunity to improve the basic American system of assisting the disabled, elderly, and others unable to work. The starting point for this approach is the fact that the program is so vital to the economic well-being of a large portion of the population. It provides at least 50 percent of income for two-thirds of the elderly; without it, almost half the elderly today would fall below the poverty line.

Given the importance and complexity of the issues involved, the Century Foundation/Twentieth Century Fund decided several years ago to support a series of studies on aspects of the aging of the population in general, and the future of Social Security in particular. We have published a number of pamphlets in our Basics series on this issue—*Social Security Reform* as well as *Medicare Reform* and *Medicaid Reform*; Malvin Schechter's book, *Beyond Medicare*; and Sylvester J. Schieber and John B. Shoven's edited volume, *Public Policy Toward Pensions*. In addition, we will soon be publishing Theda Skocpol's book on old and young in American social policy and Robert Butler's edited volume on life in an older America. Moreover, a few months ago, we published another paper by Robert Eisner: *The Great Deficit Scares: The Federal Deficit, Trade, and Social Security*.

In the pages that follow, Robert Eisner delves further into the issues surrounding Social Security, outlining his personal proposal for a significant change in the program—one that goes beyond meeting the forecasted financial needs to expand the program's value to many citizens. Eisner, professor emeritus of economics at Northwestern University, past president of the American Economic Association, and author of *The Misunderstood Economy,* as always offers provocative ideas, combining his usual elegance of economic thought with his routine boldness about policy. On behalf of the Trustees of the Century Foundation/Twentieth Century Fund, I thank him for his continuing, important contributions to this debate.

RICHARD C. LEONE, *PRESIDENT*
The Century Foundation/Twentieth Century Fund
February 1998

Contents

Acknowledgments

I am indebted to Greg Anrig, Mary Eccles, William G. Gale, Richard C. Leone, James Poterba, and Peter Wheeler for helpful comments and to Harry C. Ballantyne and various staff of the Office of the Chief Actuary of the Social Security Administration for a number of tabulations of Social Security data. Suken Shah has furnished invaluable assistance in the execution of underlying calculations and preparation of tables. Steven Greenfield has again done his usual excellent job of copyediting.

1

If It Ain't Broke, Don't Fix It! Build on It!

This is a proposal to preserve all current benefits of Social Security and to extend them. It would add to the present system, not subtract from it. It can increase the retirement benefits of most Americans. It would encourage saving. It would contribute to making the Social Security Trust Funds solvent indefinitely. It would entail no new taxes yet by current measures would cut the budget deficit or add to the surplus. And it would maintain our system of social insurance, which has served the American people so well for more than six decades.

Fear, Reality, and a Proposal

Social Security is not broke. It is not going bankrupt. It faces no crisis. The only legitimate fear is that some of those who would "reform" it would nibble away at it, if not destroy it.

But millions of elderly Americans live today in hardship, if not poverty. And a vast majority of younger Americans are correctly concerned that their retirement incomes will be inadequate. Confusion and unfounded fears for the "solvency" of Social Security have been joined by the desire to provide better for those golden years.

These fears and desires have helped fuel a drive for "privatization." Yet Social Security is by far the most successful pension and insurance system in the nation—and greater in size than all the private arrangements combined. It can be made to offer, with equity and security, larger benefits and comfortable living for the elderly. I propose adding to the Social Security system a program of voluntary, additional contributions. These would be invested in passive, indexed stock or bond funds or in Treasury securities and credited to participants' existing Social Security accounts. The Treasury securities would offer the same return as is credited to fund balances in the current system. Investment in the index funds would yield the market returns.

The contributions, like most of those to private retirement plans such as 401(k)s and IRAs, would be tax deductible, but the eventual benefits would be taxable. Unlike private plans, the supplementary Social Security program would provide actuarially fair annuities and automatic cost-of-living adjustments. And none of the potential benefits would be dissipated through the high administrative costs or the commissions and profits that figure in privatized programs.

The program of supplementary contributions would permit and encourage the accumulation of significant additional retirement income for its participants. It would help meet concerns about Social Security fund balances far into the twenty-first century. And it would facilitate increases—not decreases—in benefits in the current program.

2

What Social Security Provides Now

The Old-Age and Survivors Insurance and Disability Insurance (OASDI) program in the United States paid benefits of $347.1 billion in 1996, distributing monthly benefits to 43.7 million people at the end of the year. The mean figure for benefits provided to retired workers was slightly less than $9,000 in 1997; it is estimated to rise in 1998, on the basis of a 2.1 percent COLA (cost-of-living adjustment), to $9,180.[1] Among those receiving monthly benefits, 3 million are children under eighteen, mostly children of deceased workers, and 5 million are disabled adults.[2] The present value of the prospective Social Security payments of those over sixty-five constitutes more than half of all of their assets. And Social Security provides more than $12 trillion in life insurance protection, more than the amount of all private life insurance in force. Social Security is also credited with keeping 15 million people from falling below the poverty line and with reducing the proportion of the elderly in poverty to about 12 percent, no higher than that for other adults.

Social Security is one of the three pillars of the system by which Americans provide for their retirement years. The other two are private pension plans[3] and the various ways in which

Americans save on their own account, investing in stocks, bonds, and, of chief importance for most, their own homes. About half of those over sixty-five, however, have no claims to income other than their Social Security. Average Social Security benefits for a family with a retired worker total about $10,000.[4] The bottom fifth of Social Security households receive less than $6,000 a year, and that constitutes 81 percent of their income on average.

The situation is much worse for many older women living alone. The mean private pension for older women, as pointed out in a recent Twentieth Century Fund publication,[5] yields $3,940 annually, compared to $7,468 for men; 37 percent of older women living alone rely on their generally smaller Social Security checks for at least 90 percent of their income.

Some of the shortcomings and inequities in Social Security retirement benefits can—and should—be remedied within the existing framework. For one thing, as recommended by the 1994–1996 Advisory Council on Social Security, the structure of family benefits might be revised by guaranteeing aged survivors 75 percent of the couple's combined benefits.[6] Special attention should be given to the large numbers of impoverished, elderly women living alone. For another, all Social Security benefits not based on contributions already levied might be included in taxable income, but the gross benefits could then be increased so that mean after-tax benefits would not be reduced. This would offer some help to the poorest among the elderly. Finally, benefits might better be tied to an index of wages rather than to any measure of the cost of living, so that the elderly can share in the general gains—and occasional losses—of their working children and grandchildren. In general, benefits should be increased, not reduced, in our mighty, surging economy.

3

The Drive to "Reform" Social Security

Trust Fund "Bankruptcy" Nonsense

The intermediate projection of the Social Security trustees would have the Old-Age and Survivors Insurance and Disability Insurance (OASDI) Trust Funds short of money in thirty-one years (see Table 3.1, on page 6). "Disaster!" we are told. Our retirees at that time will no longer get their full benefits. Public opinion polls confirm the skepticism of many who say, "Social Security will not be there for us."

This is nonsense.[1] For one thing, projections three decades and more ahead are, to use a gentle word, dubious. Even relatively short-term forecasts can be notoriously inaccurate. The Congressional Budget Office (CBO), for example, in December 1995 forecast a federal deficit for fiscal year 1997 of $182 billion. It lowered it to $165 billion[2] in May 1996 and to $124 billion[3] in January of 1997. It finally revised its forecast of the 1997 federal deficit from a figure of $115 billion as late as March, when the fiscal year was already half over, to $23 billion, approximately the correct figure, in August. For whatever any such forecasts are worth, the

OASDI trustee "low-cost" Social Security projections, entailing plausible but slightly more optimistic assumptions than their intermediate forecasts about economic growth, birth rates, and immigration, foresee no shortage in the funds, as shown in Table 3.1.

Some of the economic assumptions underlying the widely cited intermediate forecasts[4] are, interestingly, already wide of the mark. Real GDP growth, for example, was forecast to be 2.5 percent in 1997 and 2.0 percent in 1998. Actual 1997 growth was 3.7 percent, and the usually conservative forecast of the CBO[5] now puts it at 2.7 percent in fiscal 1998. Unemployment was assumed to be 5.4 percent in 1997 and 5.7 percent in 1998; it actually averaged 4.9 percent in 1997 and has been forecast by the CBO to be 4.8 percent in fiscal 1998. The trustees' intermediate

Table 3.1. Intermediate- and Low-Cost Projections of OASDI Current Surpluses and Balances, Billions of Dollars

	Intermediate-Cost Projections		Low-Cost Projections	
Year	Fund Balance at Beginning of Year	Current Surplus (Net Increase in Fund Balance)	Fund Balance at Beginning of Year	Current Surplus (Net Increase in Fund Balance)
1997	567	81	567	83
1998	647	82	650	90
1999	729	86	740	100
2000	815	92	840	111
2005	1,335	124	1,535	185
2015	2,642	96	4,594	296
2018	2,869	24	—	—
2019	2,892	-10	—	—
2020	2,785	-49	5,487	289
2025	2,175	-310	6,873	253
2029	501	-613	—	—
2030	-112	-701	8,047	216
2075	-374,643	-30,678	42,895	2,061

Source: 1997 Annual Report of the Board of Trustees of the Federal Old-Age and Survivors Insurance and Disability Insurance Trust Funds, page 87, Table II.F3, and page 182, Table III.B3. Intermediate-cost projection data for years 2018, 2019, 2029, and 2030 from computer files made available by Office of the Actuary of the Social Security Administration.

forecasts put growth in the labor force at 1.1 percent for 1997; the twelve-month growth rate from December 1996 to December 1997 was actually 1.9 percent. They put the inflation rate, based on the consumer price index (CPI), at 3.2 percent through 1999, while the actual 1997 and CBO-forecast rates through 1999 now average 2.4 percent. Altering the economic assumptions to fit current realities would generally increase forecast fund balances.

But, more fundamentally, the prospective "shortage" in the Social Security Trust Funds is an accounting matter. It can be eliminated by any one of a number of simple and reasonable changes in accounting. Currently, for historical reasons and in imitation of funded, private retirement plans, there are special funds—actually government accounts—devoted to benefits with the proceeds of a dedicated tax credited to them. Actually, all "contributions for social insurance"—payroll taxes—go to the Treasury, and all benefit checks are drawn on and paid by the Treasury. As long as the payroll tax rates and the schedules of benefits remained the same, it would make no economic difference if the separate trust fund accounts were eliminated.

Some argue that it would make a political difference, that benefits are somehow more secure if they are charged to these special accounts, otherwise known as the Insurance OASDI Trust Funds. Since much of the public probably believes this and would be alarmed if the special accounts were eliminated, it is best to keep them. And it is best to continue to finance them with clearly earmarked taxes. There is no reason, though, to restrict them to the proceeds from the current 12.4 percent payroll tax.

One eminently reasonable supplement to the funds would be the portion of income tax that is currently paid on payroll tax "contributions," which are not tax deductible. The policy might go further and credit the trust funds with a specified portion of income taxes. It might make sense, for example, to dedicate to the funds a portion of those taxes equal to 1.5 percent of taxable corporate and individual income. This would correspond to the estimated 2.23 percent of taxable payroll that the "intermediate-cost" forecast of the Social Security trustees indicates would have to be added to keep the combined OASDI Trust Funds fully solvent for at least another seventy-five years.

None of this would make any real difference to the measure of the deficit, or the debt held by the public, or to the performance of the economy. It would simply entail crediting to the Social Security accounts some of what now goes to the general revenue account. Some may ask, if more revenues are credited to special accounts, will that not force the government to raise taxes or reduce outlays? The clear answer, to anyone who thinks it through, is no. Since changing the accounting would not alter total revenues or total outlays, it would have no effect on the ability to spend, tax, or borrow. No other government programs would be affected.

The trust funds are also credited with an "interest" return on their accounting balances, which is recognized in the form of nonnegotiable Treasury securities. The average rate applying to the portion of these balances that accrued in 1996 was 6.6 percent. With that rate now linked to the interest rates on marketable securities, which have been edging downward, that figure may well be lower in the future. It would be appropriate to permit the Treasury to break the link to the rate on marketable securities in order to grant these balances a higher rate of return.

Privatizers are fond of saying how much more people could earn if they did not have to pay into Social Security but instead could invest in the stock market. But mandatory contributions to Social Security are preventing the Treasury from having to borrow as much and hence permitting those who would otherwise be lending to the Treasury to invest in the stock market. The Treasury might thus reasonably bolster the trust fund balances with at least a few percentage points more of "interest." Again, this would be merely a matter of bookkeeping, not affecting the debt held by the public, or the deficit, or the benefits paid out by Social Security. It would only change what the accountants are crediting to the funds and hence their balances.

Since the trust fund accounts must apparently be maintained for political reasons and in the interest of public confidence, it would be useful to adopt one or several of the measures just indicated to keep the accounts "solvent" into the indefinite future. But any forecasts of future shortfalls in these accounts are in no way a justification and should not be an excuse for either reducing benefits or raising taxes.

Suppose, for example, there were a separate account for National Defense to which the corporate income tax was dedicated. Note then that corporate income tax receipts are currently about $210 billion while defense outlays run at more than a $250 billion annual rate. There may well be good reasons to cut defense expenditures, but the shortfall of revenues in a "National Defense Trust Fund" would hardly be one of them.

THE "MONEY'S WORTH" ISSUE

A second bit of nonsense about Social Security is that beneficiaries will not be getting their "money's worth" for their contributions. This refers to calculating the payroll taxes put in by contributors and relating these to their ultimate benefits. This is not a meaningful comparison to begin with, but it is frequently not even done right. The measure of benefits should properly include not merely retirement but disability and survivor payments as well. The disability insurance in Social Security has been estimated to be equivalent to a $207,000 policy in the private sector. And a comparable dependent and survivor policy for a twenty-seven-year-old, average-wage worker with two small children would cost $307,000.[6]

But all payroll taxes, regardless of where the accountants credit them, go into the general Treasury pot, along with all other government revenues, and all benefits, along with all other payments, come out of that same pot.[7] Relating benefits to payroll taxes alone is thus a meaningless calculation.

One might properly undertake the complex task of relating all of what each American receives from government to all that he or she gives. This would include police and defense and education and health services along with interest payments on the debt, and Social Security and other "transfer payments." If national defense outlays were apportioned on the basis of the wealth and property being "defended," it might reveal some surprising results, showing that while the wealthy do pay more in taxes they also get much more in the way of government services.

As far as Social Security goes, though, it is true that upper-income groups receive much less in comparison to their earnings—and their (irrelevant) payroll taxes—than do the poor. The formula is stacked so that monthly benefits equal the total of 90 percent of the first $455 of "average indexed monthly earnings," 32 percent of the amount between $455 and $2,471, and only 15 percent of the amount in excess of $2,471.

The wealthy and many in the upper middle class may well complain that they are not getting that much out of Social Security. If they could have back their payroll tax contributions and invest them in the stock market, even leaving aside the boom of the past several years, some of them argue, they would be better off.

But Social Security was not meant to be a get-rich scheme or a competitor to go-go investment funds. It is social insurance. It is meant to provide at least a minimum standard of support for all, regardless of initial station or life's vicissitudes. Those who have good fortune will be able to say in hindsight that they did not need it, just as does the individual who buys insurance on her house and never sees it burn down, or one who buys life insurance to benefit his young spouse and children and then lives to ninety.

Social Security in the United States is incredibly efficient, in the sense that its administrative costs, amounting to some 0.8 percent of payouts,[8] are infinitesimal compared to those of private insurance. And Social Security provides vital benefits such as cost-of-living adjustments and actuarially fair annuities that private insurance can hardly begin to offer.

Automatic cost-of-living adjustments are currently available in only 3 percent of private pension plans.[9] The failure to offer such guarantees against erosion of benefits relates to the risk endemic to private plans. Until the recent introduction of inflation-indexed U.S. Treasury securities, private plans could not find assets offering real returns that could finance inflation-protected benefits. Even now, the real rate of interest offered on such securities, about 3.7 percent as of February 1998, would finance retirement annuities considerably lower than those otherwise available from a broader mix of investments, including corporate bonds and equities.

Private, actuarially fair annuities are also not available for reasons that are inherent in private markets. A careful and authoritative study reported in a recent National Bureau of Economic Research Working Paper finds: "The average sixty-five-year-old contemplating the purchase of a life annuity, whose alternative is a Treasury bond, receives payouts with a present value of 80 to 85 cents per dollar of premiums. The remaining premium dollars must cover marketing costs, corporate overhead and income taxes, additions to various company contingency reserves, and profits, as well as the cost of adverse selection."[10] The study calculates after-tax annuity values per premium dollar for a sixty-five-year-old, on the basis of Treasury yield curves or higher corporate yield curves, as shown in Table 3.2.

The authors point out, moreover, that "joint and survivor" figures would be less if account were taken of the fact that life expectancies of spouses are positively correlated. Clearly, as they put it, "a typical retiree with average mortality prospects faces a significant 'transaction cost' if he purchases an individual annuity from a commercial insurance carrier." Similar costs apply to annuities that may be offered by 401(k) plan providers. The authors note further that the values per dollar of premium vary widely among insurers, so that the average sixty-five-year-old has a further cost of shopping to avoid coming away with less than average returns.

Table 3.2. After-Tax Annuity Values per Premium Dollar for a Sixty-Five-Year-Old

	Treasury Yield Curve	Corporate Yield Curve
Men	0.814	0.756
Women	0.854	0.785
Joint and Survivor	0.868	0.792

Source: Olivia S. Mitchell, James M. Poterba, and Mark J. Warshawsky, "New Evidence on the Money's Worth of Individual Annuities," NBER Working Paper no. 6002, National Bureau of Economic Research, Cambridge, Mass., April 1997, p. 2.

As compared to private retirement plans, then, Social Security is certainly overall the best buy in town.

THE BURDEN OF THE AGING BABY BOOMERS

There is a third issue, this one a legitimate concern, regarding the impact on Social Security of the aging generation of baby boomers. The ratio of the population that is past retirement age to those of working age—twenty to sixty-four—will be growing. In this regard, there are now almost five people of working age for every potential dependent aged sixty-five and over, but by the year 2030 that ratio will fall to less than three-to-one.

The relevant numbers, though, relate to all potential dependents, the young—under twenty years of age—as well as the old. In 1995, for every 1,000 people of working age there were 710 young and old potential dependents. The intermediate projection puts the number of potential dependents in the year 2030 at 788.[11] This means that those 1,000 people of working age would have to support 1,788 people—themselves and their dependents—instead of 1,710, a 4.56 percent increase in their burden.

But if productivity per worker grows at a modest 1 percent per year, well within historical experience, the growth in total output per worker will have come to more than 40 percent by the year 2030. This would increase income per capita by more than a third, ample to improve vastly the lot of all—the elderly, the young, and those in their working prime.

An increase in the aged dependency ratio—putting aside for the moment a decrease in the under-twenty dependency ratio—will require those in the twenty-to-sixty-four age group, the working population, to devote a greater share of their increasing incomes to supporting those sixty-five and over. But this support must be current. The only way to provide for the future is to provide physical or, more important, human capital that will be productive in the future. That means more productive investment, public and private, and more and better educated and trained workers in the future. Of course, more births and more immigration would help.

But neither putting more money in Social Security nor increasing financial investment in the stockmarket or elsewhere in themselves put any food on future tables. The frequent characterization of pay-as-you-go financing in Social Security, as a Ponzi scheme, in which each generation is borrowing from the succeeding generation, which will in turn borrow from its successors, is inaccurate. One generation takes from its successors only by consuming or not providing the capital, physical and human, that will provide for future production. While we can save and invest now in more ovens that will be useful at a future time, the bread dependents eat at any time must be baked by those working then. Retirees cannot eat balances in Social Security Trust Funds, or stocks and bonds, or cash. In a real sense, for the economy as a whole, retirement benefits are thus always supplied on a pay-as-you-go basis.

That is why it makes perfect sense to finance Social Security on a pay-as-you-go basis, raising taxes on the working population to finance benefits for the increasing proportions of the aged as those increases occur. But then it must be recognized that this relative aging about which there has been so much comment is still well off in the future. The aged dependency ratio, 21.4 percent in 1995, will, according to the intermediate forecast of the Social Security trustees, actually decline to 21.1 percent in 2000 and to 20.7 percent in 2005 before finally returning to 21.4 percent in 2010. There is hence no need whatsoever to raise taxes or cut benefits to the elderly over the next twelve years. If there is a problem with rising dependency ratios, it is not a short-run or even an intermediate-run difficulty.

What proportions of increasing incomes and output must go to support the growing ranks of the elderly when those numbers do swell—assuming we want to maintain both the working and the elderly populations in the same relative position? With an elder dependency ratio of 0.214 in 1995, each 1,000 people of working age needed to support 1,214—themselves and 214 elderly. If the dependency ratio rises to 0.239 in the year 2015, as is forecast, each 1,000 people of working age will have to support 1,239 adults in all. Their burden will thus have increased by roughly 2 percent.

It follows that the real per capita incomes of, or the goods and services available to, both the working population and the elderly will be reduced by 2 percent from what they would have been if the elder dependency ratio had not risen. To avoid inflation in this circumstance, purchasing power overall should be reduced by 2 percent. For the working population, this may be accomplished by increasing their taxes by 2 percent of their incomes; for the elderly, we may cut retirement benefits by a corresponding amount or, in order to keep matters fully symmetrical, increase their income taxes by 2 percent of their total incomes as well.

By the year 2020, when the aged dependency ratio is up to 0.275 and the burden per 1,000 workers thus is up to 1,275, or 4.98 percent above the burden in 1995, net incomes per capita of the working population and the elderly will be 4.7 percent less than they would have been without the increase in the dependency ratio, as shown in Table 3.3.[12] In 2025, net incomes will be 7.9 percent less. In 2030, the year of the alleged apocalypse when the trust funds will no longer be able to finance all currently legislated benefits, net incomes will be 10.4 percent less. If the forecasts are correct, by 2075, seventy-seven years from now, net incomes per capita will be 14.2 percent less.

But these cuts in net income per capita are all relative. If the average income per worker increases at even a very modest 1 percent a year, then even with the reductions in net income per capita, everybody—the young, the working population, and the aged—will still be able to enjoy higher absolute incomes and be far better off than today. In 2030, per capita income would be 26.9 percent more, and in 2075 it would be 90.2 percent more, as Table 3.3 clearly shows. There is no reason why retirees should not be permitted to share proportionately in these gains.

With increasing proportions of income appearing in forms other than wages, it makes more sense than ever to finance Social Security, if it is to have a dedicated tax, with a portion of income taxes. Policymakers could drop all of the 12.4 percent tax on payrolls and substitute an increase of about 8.3 percentage points in the average taxation of individual and corporate income, specifically earmarked, as are payroll taxes now, for the Social Security Trust Funds. It is appropriate for those who earn income without working, as well as those who earn from working, both to contribute to and to receive benefits from Social Security.[13]

Table 3.3. Changes in Aged Dependency Ratios and Net Incomes Per Capita

Year	Aged Dependency Ratio*	Burden per Worker (1 + Dependency Ratio) as Percentage of 1995	Percent Change in Net Income per Capita Because of Increase in Dependency Ratio	Percentage Increase in Net Income per Worker from 1 Percent per Annum Growth	Percentage Net Change in Income per Capita
1995	0.214	100.0	—	—	—
2000	0.211	99.8	+0.2	5.1	+5.4
2005	0.207	99.4	+0.5	10.5	+11.0
2010	0.214	100.0	—	16.1	+16.1
2015	0.239	102.05	-2.0	22.0	+19.6
2020	0.275	104.98	-4.7	28.2	+22.2
2025	0.319	108.61	-7.9	34.8	+24.1
2030	0.355	111.61	-10.4	41.7	+26.9
2075	0.415	116.56	-14.2	121.7	+90.2

* From *1997 Annual Report of the Board of Trustees of the Federal Old-Age and Survivors Insurance and Disability Insurance Trust Funds*, Table II.H1, p. 148.

Nibbling Away at Social Security

Recent arguments that the consumer price index is overstating inflation have generated new suggestions that cost-of-living adjustments for those on Social Security be reduced to correspond to a new, corrected CPI. The widely mentioned 1.1 percent per year correction[14] would result in trimming benefits by some 10 percent (relative to the arrangement now in place) over the average twenty-year period in which retirees enjoy benefits.

I would go the other way and end the squabble about the cost-of-living adjustment by indexing benefits to wages rather than prices. Retirees would share in growing productivity and the rising real wages of those working but would also share in any sacrifice if higher prices of imports, such as those sparked in the past by drastic increases in oil prices, leave everyone with less output for domestic needs. This would mean that retirees would share in the gains—and occasional losses—of their working sons and daughters. With real wages rising by 0.9 percent per year, as projected in the OASDI intermediate forecast, shifting the index of adjustment after retirement from prices to wages would increase benefits by that amount, or some 10 percent over the life of the average retiree.

I would also remedy the situation by which second income earners add little to a couple's prospective retirement benefits over and above the 50 percent spousal benefits already provided. Under current law, if that second wage earner, usually a woman, is entitled on the basis of her own earnings to benefits worth less than 50 percent of the benefits that would be received by her husband if he were single, the couple will get no more than if she had not worked at all. All of her payroll tax contributions will have been for naught. But I would not use "reform" as a pretext to nibble away at Social Security or to destroy it. Even some of its defenders seem all too ready to accept "minor" cuts in benefits to achieve prospective fund balance. One of the more insidious and drastic "solutions" is to postpone further the "normal retirement age," already slated to rise gradually in future years from sixty-five to sixty-seven.

Actually, this has nothing to do with encouraging people to work longer. They already have that encouragement since benefits increase if those over sixty-five work longer (up to the age of seventy) and are cut if they retire earlier. Currently, retirement at sixty-five provides 100 percent of benefits; 4.5 percentage points are added for each year retirement is delayed, up to age seventy, at which point annual benefits would be 122.5 percent of the norm.

Early retirement, at age sixty-two, by contrast, results in annual benefits only 80 percent of the standard retirement level. A higher "normal retirement age" would merely lower the entire scale of benefits. If, for example, this were raised to age seventy, those retiring subsequently would get the same annual benefits that people now claim at age sixty-five, that is, some 18 percent less than a newly retired seventy-year-old currently receives. Those retiring at age sixty-two would get still less, perhaps 70 percent instead of 80 percent of the benefits that people now get at age sixty-five.[15]

What's Wrong with "Privatization"

Some "reformers" would move to partial or complete "privatization." They would have all or part of current contributions diverted from the trust funds and used instead to buy stocks and bonds. These would be owned by the individual investors and would be a substitute for Social Security. Those whose incomes are high enough for them to have much to invest and those who are fortunate in their investments will do well. But the social insurance aspect of Social Security would be lost. Those lower on the income scale or whose earning power was damaged by mishap would be major losers, unless added benefits were provided by the Treasury. Clearly, those who do not know how to invest wisely would suffer as well.

Private investment is generally unable to provide guaranteed protection against inflation. As indicated above, the new indexed Treasury bonds would do so only at low returns. And private investment or insurance does not, and cannot because of the risks involved, offer anywhere near actuarially fair annuities. Even if an elderly retiree has managed to make substantial and fortunate investment with a significant nest egg over his career, that lump sum cannot be converted to secure and adequate real returns for himself and his spouse over the rest of their lives.

Full privatization of all or any part of Social Security would entail costs that would significantly reduce net returns and benefits. Mean payroll tax contributions to Social Security were about $220 per month in 1996. If 5 percentage points of the 12.4 percent payroll tax were diverted to private investment, as advocated in the "personal security account" proposal put forth by five members of the twelve-person Advisory Council on Social Security,[16] that would come to an average of around $100. Imagine brokers or mutual funds handling monthly investments in amounts that would be this small (and for many of the 150 million covered workers much less still) and then making monthly payments to as many as 50 million retirees. For those that would be willing to handle such small accounts, service charges would have to be large.[17]

Privatization would also create major transition problems. The substantial annual surplus in the trust funds notwithstanding, in the present pay-as-you-go system, current contributors in effect pay for current benefits. If current contributions are used instead to buy stocks and bonds for the contributors, the shortfall for covering current retirees' benefits has to be made up somehow. This could be done by more explicit borrowing from the public, thus raising the nation's budget deficit. Or it could be made up by increased taxes, which would weaken purchasing power and slow the economy.

Underlying the current debate about Social Security are real issues about the distribution of income and wealth, between rich and poor, between the young and the elderly, and between those working and those not working. And there is much ideologically driven passion regarding the part government plays in the resolution of these issues. Some believe that all should be left to private decisions and private markets, whatever the consequences. Others look for a greater role for government in providing the social insurance that is beyond the capacity of individuals or corporations. In the last analysis it is hard for most to contemplate a society in which people, whether through their own mistakes or inadequacies or societally inflicted misfortunes, are starving in the street.

Most of us, therefore, recognize the wisdom of mandating contributions toward providing at least a minimum set of benefits sufficient to insure all against destitution. That is what the current Social Security system has sought to achieve—and it has, to a considerable extent, succeeded. It also is widely recognized, though, that the system should facilitate individuals' free, private decisions to reach beyond these minimum benefits when they can.

4

A Change for the Better

Voluntary Supplementary Contributions to Social Security

All current benefits of Social Security should be preserved and extended. Rather than diminishing Social Security by privatizing it, I propose greater public provision of benefits on the basis of voluntary, supplementary contributions to the trust funds. I would add to our present public system, not subtract from it. For those concerned about the trust funds, implementation of my proposal can contribute to making them solvent indefinitely but will entail no new taxes. It will offer additional inducements to save. Most important, it can increase the retirement benefits of most Americans.

Millions of workers do not have access to 401(k)s or private pension funds at work. Those who contribute to individual retirement accounts (IRAs) are generally limited to $2,000 per year per person. Many would at various times, if not steadily, contribute more to retirement were an appropriate vehicle, particularly a tax-exempt one, available.

But millions of Americans—and it is easy to underestimate their number—are unsophisticated in the ways of private investment and uncertain and fearful about the risks. Despite all the unfortunate doubts and cynicism about its reliability, Social Security is the best game in town in the eyes of millions of Americans who have seen their parents and grandparents saved from poverty.

If a voluntary, supplementary Social Security program with a few simple options were put into operation, and if it were adequately publicized, it seems reasonable to believe that it would become enormously popular. For those anxious to minimize risk, an option of investment in Treasury securities would be attractive. For the more ambitious, looking for somewhat higher returns, a bond index fund could be made available. For those still more adventurous, hoping for even higher returns, there could be a passive stock index fund. And all could have the actuarially fair annuities and cost-of-living adjustments not available in the private market.

My basic proposal is simple, although there can be various useful elaborations and corollaries. All participants in the Social Security system—which should be as universal as possible[1]—should be offered the opportunity, but not compelled, to make supplementary contributions to the trust funds, and those contributions would be credited to their own individual accounts. Unlike current, required employee payroll contributions, but like most contributions to private pension plans, they would be tax deductible. Interest or other income earned on the supplemental balances would also be tax-exempt, but the resulting additions to retirement income, as with most private pensions,[2] would be taxable.

Unlike many private pension arrangements, however, while there would be benefits for the survivors of those who die before retirement and, to some extent, for survivors of those who die early in their retirement years, contributors would not be permitted to cash out their investments. This is important to keep the program focused on supplementing retirement benefits rather than merely offering new channels of investment. It is also important to minimize the role of adverse selection, which would complicate the provision of actuarially fair benefits.[3]

Contributors to supplementary accounts would have a choice of the following investments: 1) a fully passive stock index fund; 2) a fully passive bond index fund; 3) Treasury securities; 4) any combination of the above. The returns on these investments would be credited to the OASDI Trust Funds but earmarked to the individual accounts of the investors. The new accounts would represent *public* counterparts of private Keogh plans, IRAs, and 401(k)s, 403(b)s, and 457s.[4] They would have significant advantages over what is provided in existing private plans.

The consolidation of investments in a minimum number of funds or securities and of supplemental accounts in the already existing Social Security system would offer major savings as compared with the administrative costs, commissions, and profits that eat into net private returns. The public system would offer actuarially fair benefits from the accumulations available at retirement; it would offer automatic cost-of-living adjustments; and it would offer appealing new opportunities to millions of Americans unsophisticated in the ways of Wall Street and fearful, often justifiably so, of the siren songs of those who would take their money.

The public investments would thus be highly desirable to many, both as supplements to and, if need be, substitutes for employer pension plans[5] and individual retirement accounts. They would also draw in funds from those who have tried to provide for their retirement by way of uncertain individual investments that do not offer annuities. And they might attract entirely new saving from many who would find these new options sufficiently attractive to warrant the sacrifice of present consumption in the interest of more for their golden years.

It might be deemed judicious to put an upper limit on the amount of tax-deductible contributions to prevent the very rich from using these contributions to make a mockery of the progressivity of the income tax. If so, however, I would urge that the ceiling should be high—perhaps identical to the $9,500 of 401(k) contributions—so that the new investments offer opportunities for higher-income participants to do substantially more than move savings from existing pension and retirement plans.

While the increased tax deductions would cause some initial loss in income tax revenues, the Treasury and the trust funds would eventually gain much more through the inflow of the supplementary contributions or the income they generate and through the taxes on benefits. The initial loss to the Treasury might be made less by restricting the tax deductibility of these contributions to

$2,000 per person, the current upper limit on IRA contributions, rather than the higher 401(k) limit suggested above. The limit might then rise over time with an index for inflation.

I would predict that, with sufficient publicity, many millions of participants in the Social Security system would make major voluntary, additional contributions and would significantly raise their prospective retirement income. Just how much they would gain clearly would depend upon how much they contribute and how well their investments perform.

The Specifics

How all this would work may be shown with projections derived from elementary assumptions that, however simple, capture the essence of my proposal.

1. All covered workers in Social Security will be given the opportunity to make additional contributions that they can designate to be invested in Treasury securities or in a bond or stock index fund to be bought by the Old-Age and Survivors Insurance (OASI) Trust Fund. These extra contributions will be tax deductible, but ultimately the benefits received from them will be taxable. I assume an average marginal tax rate of 20 percent.

2. Participants in this Supplementary Social Security program who choose to invest in Treasury securities would have their balances credited at the same rates as the basic Social Security balances.[6] To the extent they select indexed stock or bond funds they will be credited with whatever return those funds earn.

3. I will assume that the program begins in 1998. To facilitate projections of results, I shall present a model built on a number of simplifying assumptions. First, all cohorts from the age of thirty-five to sixty-four shall be eligible to contribute, and all benefits will begin at age sixty-five and be paid for twenty years. Those born in 1934 will thus be the oldest to participate. They will be able to contribute for only one year and will then

begin to receive benefits. The 1963 cohort will be the first one with the opportunity to contribute for a full thirty years.

I shall assume further, to make the calculations easy, that each cohort's size remains the same after it enters the program; this could be taken to mean that everybody lives eighty-five years and that death comes on one's eighty-fifth birthday, with no survivor benefits. Alternatively, it can be taken to mean that the assumption of no change in cohort size, at least after retirement, reflects the benefits received by survivors. And I shall assume that the cohorts aged thirty-five to sixty-four account for all of the projected taxable payroll of $3,350 billion and the 147 million covered workers in 1998.

These assumptions and parameters, while arbitrary, facilitate the illustrations. Results should not be expected to differ fundamentally if contributions could be made at any age and if ages of death and retirement varied from individual to individual and from cohort to cohort.

4. In my first illustration, the mean supplementary contribution will be 3.1 percent of taxable payroll, thus adding 50 percent to the current mandatory employee contribution of 6.2 percent of taxable wages. This additional contribution in 1998 would average $706 per person, and with about 147 million contributors in the program, it would come to a total of $103.85 billion. Each individual's contributions will increase by 3.96 percent per year thereafter, slightly less than the forecast mean per annum rate of increase of 4.39 percent from 1998 to 2075 of the Social Security Administration average wage index. Taking into account a projected rate of growth of cohort size of 1 percent per year, the forecast rate of increase of aggregate wages—and I presume GDP as well—is then 5 percent per year,[7] very close to the OASDI projection of 4.87 percent.

   In alternate simulations I will assume that each individual's contribution will increase by only the amount of the OASDI intermediate forecast of a 0.9 percent per annum increase in real wages, adjusted for the rate of inflation, and that the growth in cohort size will follow the OASDI projections for the population aged twenty to sixty-four. Since this growth is expected to slow markedly from about 1 percent per annum over the next two decades, approximating zero after thirty years, the growth in contributions will slow as well, from an initial 4.79 percent to 4.20 percent by 2025 and to 4.13 percent by 2047.

While the OASDI intermediate forecast sets the long-range inflation rate at 3.5 percent,[8] I assume initially yearly inflation of 2.5 percent, closer to the rate implied by the difference between interest rates on conventional bonds and on the new, inflation-indexed Treasury securities[9] (and still above the 2.1 percent rate registered over the past year). I shall also, however, demonstrate the effects of rates of inflation held constant at both 2.1 percent and 3.5 percent.

The OASDI intermediate forecast, as indicated above, sets the per annum, long-run increase in real wages at 0.9 percent. I hope and believe that this forecast is unduly pessimistic. But total wages covered in payrolls will also increase as a consequence of the rising upper limit on taxable wages per worker. The assumptions of 2.5 percent price inflation and a 3.96 percent increase in contributions based on wages do not therefore necessarily imply an increase in real hourly wage rates of 1.4 percent per year, which would conflict with the OASDI assumption as to real wage growth. I shall, however, model some alternative assumptions, particularly on the premise that the increase in total wages is slowed in future years by decelerating growth in the size of the working-age population.

5. I shall assume initially that the indexed funds actually earn 8 percent per year, which is credited to the individual accounts. I shall then note the implications of different rates of return on these funds, and I will give consideration to those that put their supplementary contributions into Treasury securities as well.

6. Benefits will be paid on an actuarially fair basis over the twenty-year retirement period,with the assumed rate of return credited on the remaining balance throughout the span. Initial payments will be scaled down to accommodate the cost-of-living adjustment. The balance at the end of the twenty-year period will thus be zero.

retirement thus necessitates a reduction in real benefits. For those contributing for the full thirty years, benefits in 1998 dollars of $4,567, with my originally assumed inflation rate of 2.5 percent, are reduced to $3,539 if the OASDI projection of a 3.5 percent inflation rate in the future turns out to be correct. Real benefits would be raised to $5,066 if the current 2.1 percent cost-of-living adjustment for 1998 were repeated indefinitely into the future. The reduction in real benefits associated with greater rates of inflation could be avoided if the Social Security system—in effect, the U.S. Treasury—were to undertake to finance whatever cost-of-living adjustment is indicated by the consumer price index, as it does with current benefits. My proposal might well be modified to encompass this.

The reduction in real benefits accompanying greater inflation rates in my simulations follows as well, however, from the assumption that nominal rates of return are not affected. This implies that real rates of return are reduced proportionately by higher rates of inflation. It would seem more reasonable to assume that over the long run real rates of return are not affected by inflation. This would mean that if a 3.5 percent inflation rate is assumed, for example, instead of 2.5 percent, it would be appropriate to expect a nominal stock index return of 9.05 percent[3] instead of 8 percent and have the Treasury credit fund balances at 9.05 percent for investment in Treasury securities. Such a nominal rate of return is of course still far below what has been enjoyed on average in the stockmarket in recent years.[4]

As shown in Table 5.3, crediting the higher rate of return would restore the real benefits lost to inflation. The Treasury might, alternatively, each year adjust the rate of interest credited to the funds by the difference between the actual rate of inflation and the 2.5 percent that I have assumed in my main simulations.

It must also be noted in Table 5.3, however, that the faster rate of growth of real wages of 1.425 percent assumed in Table 5.1 generates higher real benefits. These would be $4,848 for those contributing for thirty years as against the $4,567 for the slower real wage growth of 0.9 percent and the same 2.5 percent rate of inflation.

Other Consequences: The Trust Fund

Improved Social Security retirement benefits are the most significant result of the supplementary contributions. Implementation of this proposal will have other, salutary effects on the various (real or more typically imagined) problems popularly perceived with regard to the Social Security Trust Funds, the federal budget deficit, the federal debt held by the public, and national saving. These effects are largely matters of accounting, of doubtful or nonexistent consequence. But since so many would base policy on these bookkeeping measures, they are worth noting.

These other, broad-scale implications will depend upon the rate of growth of aggregate contributions. This, in turn, will depend upon the growth in the nominal wage base for each cohort and on the rate of increase in cohort size. With my initial assumptions of a 3.96 percent per annum increase in wage base within each cohort and a 1 percent per annum increase in cohort size, aggregate contributions expand by 5 percent per year. Assume that GDP grows at this same 5 percent rate.

As shown in Table 5.2, which is built on these assumptions, fund assets immediately begin growing. By the year 2002 they will have added $689 billion to Social Security assets, equivalent to some 6.6 percent of GDP (Appendix Table A1 on pages 45–47 provides projections for all of the years from 1998 to 2058 and for 2070 and 2075). By the critical year 2029, when the intermediate-cost projection would have the OASDI combined assets on current policies exhausted, the supplementary accounts would have put $16,290 billion, or 41.6 percent of GDP, into the coffers. When equilibrium is reached in 2047, the additional fund assets of $43,450 billion will constitute 46.1 percent of GDP, and they will continue to grow in step with GDP thereafter.

What does this do to the overall shortage in the OASDI Trust Funds? The current intermediate-cost forecast for 2047 is a negative $36,605 billion. The additional assets from the supplementary contributions and the return on them will turn that negative figure to a positive $6,845 billion. The year 2052 would, however, be the last year of "solvency," even with the supplementary contributions added in. The total assets by that year would have fallen to minus $55,086 billion plus $55,455 billion supplementary, or $369 billion. In 2053 the total will have turned to a negative $2,527 billion.

For those concerned with the matter of trust fund assets, it is worth noting that, without any other corrective measure, these supplementary contributions averaging 3.1 percent of taxable wages would have put off the day of reckoning twenty-three years, from 2029 to 2052. And if supplementary contributions came to 7.3768 percent of wages, the funds would remain solvent until 2075, the end of the period of long-run forecasts.

How can larger contributions add so much to OASDI assets when they must be used to pay out increased benefits? The explanation is simple. The contributions come first while the payouts come later. There is a fifty-year transition period, until all those making the supplementary contributions are matched by those receiving benefits. Until 2047, then, it is clear that OASDI assets deriving from the supplementary contribution program will be mounting.

What may not be so obvious, though, is that even after 2047, for the indefinite future those assets will keep increasing, actually at the rate of increase of taxable payrolls. This increase occurs despite the fact that retirement annuities are actuarially fair—the individual gets back exactly what he or she has put in plus the 8 percent annual return. In the aggregate, the funds keep growing because in a growing population and expanding economy current benefits are tied to the lesser per person prior contributions of less numerous cohorts. There are more current contributors per cohort in each year than there are beneficiaries, and they are earning more, thanks to the increase in nominal wages. Only in the event that cohort size stopped growing, and in the more unlikely event that the average nominal wage base per worker stopped increasing, would the fund balances stop growing.[5]

The Federal Budget

As for the overall federal budget, as it is currently reported, the initial effect of indexed fund investment will be to increase the deficit—or reduce the surplus. These results, however, will quickly be reversed as the funds swell. The deficit rises at first because the tax-deductible supplementary contributions will go not to the Treasury but to buy the indexed stock and bond fund securities. Owing to the loss of tax receipts, with contributions of 3.1 percent of taxable payrolls the deficit will be increased by $16.4 billion or 0.19 percent of GDP in 1998. This deficit will soon be wiped out, though, as balances accumulate, assuming the returns on the indexed funds are actually 8 percent.[6] The initially very small new benefits paid out will add to the deficit but will be compensated for in minor part by the taxes paid on these benefits. By 2000 the additional income from the securities investments will be sufficient to compensate for the losses to the Treasury, and the net effect on the budget will be approximately nil.

Thereafter, the contributions to reducing the budget deficit or increasing the surplus rise rapidly. In 2002, with $48 billion in income from the investments, the net effect on the budget is $21 billion on the positive side of the ledger, or 0.20 percent of GDP. In 2010 it is $145 billion or 0.94 percent of GDP. In 2025, when the net impact on income tax payments has just turned positive, since taxable current benefits begin to exceed tax-deductible current contributions, the budget deficit is reduced or surplus increased by $555 billion or 1.72 percent of GDP.[7] While benefit payments as a percentage of GDP continue to increase, the deficit reduction or surplus enhancement as a percentage of GDP begins to fall from its maximum of 1.73 percent attained in 2026. It reaches an equilibrium value of 1.38 percent in 2047, and the dollar amount of that deficit reduction or surplus increase, then $1,304 billion, continues to grow at the 5 percent rate assumed for the growth in taxable payrolls.

To the extent that the Treasury collects the cash dividends or interest payments earned on the indexed funds, in effect borrowing from the trust funds as it does currently, it reduces its borrowing from the public. This then keeps down the most significant measure of the federal debt, that held by the public, currently some $3.8 trillion.

All of these effects on deficits and debt may indeed seem strange. One must start, however, from the strange ways in which federal government accounts are reckoned. Washington's measures are often arbitrary and not infrequently foolish. Sales of assets are netted against outlays and hence reduce the deficit.[8] When a government agency buys financial assets, such as those related to failed savings and loan institutions a few years ago, that increases the deficit; when the financial assets are sold, the deficit is reduced. Most relevant here, the addition to explicit debt enlarges the deficit while the implicit or "contingent" debt of future Social Security commitments is not counted. Hence, if government increased mandatory contributions in the form of payroll taxes and simultaneously legislated increases in future benefits, that would reduce the deficit because the increased obligation toward future benefits would not be counted. To take the position, as in this paper, that the increased voluntary contributions and the returns that accumulate on them should be considered as reducing the deficit is thus consistent with current accounting practice.

One could go the other way and view current mandatory payroll "contributions" not as taxes but as forced loans to the Treasury that will be paid back eventually in annuities.[9] If so, the conventional measure of the current deficit would be vastly increased.

In any event, my supplementary contributions and benefits would appear to offer no fundamental difference in terms of budgetary impact from the current, mandatory contributions. It is true that the benefits are more sharply defined as relating precisely to contributions, but, as with the current system, these benefits are not written in stone. Annuities might be altered on the basis of changes in life expectancy or even changes in administrative costs if Congress decided to take those into account.

National Saving

And what about the much-watched though also defective measures of "national saving"? The conventional tally adds together private saving—the sum of personal saving and the undistributed profits that constitute corporate saving—and public saving, taken as the sum of federal, state, and local budget surpluses. National saving in turn is identical, except for (recently sizable) "statistical discrepancies" in measurement, to the sum of gross private domestic investment and net foreign investment.[10] To the extent that the increased contributions to Social Security are not a substitute for other saving or investment and hence actually reduce individual consumption, they increase private saving.

How much such diversion from other saving outlets there will be, as opposed to new saving by individuals, is hard to determine. Households' and nonprofit organizations' direct holdings of corporate equity at the end of the second quarter of 1997 came to almost $5.4 trillion,[11] some of which might well be sold in order to make additional contributions to Social Security. And pension funds currently have more than $5 trillion in assets,[12] with new contributions running at a rate of some $250 billion per year.[13] IRAs had $1 trillion in assets and 401(k)s had $650 billion at the end of 1995.[14] Average contributions for the 23 million-plus participants in 401(k) plans in 1993 were almost exactly $3,000.[15] Yet calculations from a Health and Retirement Survey database indicate that 44 percent of the population have made no arrangement whatsoever for retirement saving. The percentages of Americans without such provision were put at about 64 percent for those with incomes less than $20,000 and 51 percent for those with incomes between $20,000 and $30,000.[16]

It has been estimated that close to 30 percent of married households are not saving adequately for retirement, and the median shortfall in retirement wealth is $22,480, which could be met by saving 0.52 percent of annual earnings.[17] The measure of adequacy, however, is tied to a level of income that was enjoyed prior to retirement. Many may aspire to live more than "adequately" in their final years.

My assumption that the total of voluntary contributions would amount to 3.1 percent of taxable payroll implies an aggregate of $103.85 billion in 1998. In view of what has just been discussed, this total, which translates initially as mean individual voluntary contributions of $706, does not appear unreasonable. To the extent that the actual figures were to turn out lower—or higher—my aggregate projections would be altered proportionately, but the thrust of the results would not be changed.[18]

Studies of the extent to which the introduction of 401(k)s and IRAs brought in new saving rather than a shifting of existing assets have produced disparate results. I will apply the principle of "equal ignorance" with regard to my proposed new Social Security vehicle. I will suggest that the supplementary contributions may come half from new saving and half from diversion from other methods of saving.

All this, I must caution, relates to individual efforts to save. These efforts may not in the end yield increased national saving. Household cuts in consumption may cause businesses to cut back production and reduce, rather than raise, their capital expenditures or investment as well. There would then be an associated fall in national income and saving. The advocates of increased private saving generally ignore or downplay this "Keynesian" concern, however, and may welcome the supplementary contributions as likely to increase private saving. The reduction in federal deficits, unless it is matched by increases in deficits or decreases in surpluses at the state and local level,[19] will by definition increase public saving, as conventionally measured. The ultimate effect on national saving and investment will depend on the balance of changes in public and private investment.[20]

Investment in Treasury Securities

All of the results above hold for supplementary contributions to investment in Treasury securities except those for the budget balance. To the extent that supplementary contributors use the option of investing in Treasury securities, the effects on the measured federal deficit or surplus will be somewhat different. With identical rates of return, retirement benefits will be the same regardless of the type of investment. The effects on the OASDI balances will also be the same, but the effects on the budgetary position and the Treasury debt held by the public will, because of the curiosities of federal accounting, be different.

The reason for this is that contributions used to buy Treasury securities to be held by the OASDI will, in accordance with Treasury accounting, be viewed (properly) as Treasury revenues, trimming the deficit. Debt held by the public will be correspondingly reduced since the Treasury will not have to borrow from the public amounts equal to the securities it sells to the OASDI. This will also entail savings in net interest paid by the Treasury.

OASDI purchase of indexed stock or bond funds with the supplementary contributions, on the other hand, aside from the tax deductions provided, will initially have no impact on any measured deficit or debt held by the public. However, the returns from these investments, while credited to the individual participant accounts, to the extent they are in cash or converted to cash, will flow into the Treasury and hence affect budgetary balance.

The impact on the federal budget of the two kinds of investment will be different in the fifty-year transition period, until there is a full set of those contributing all of their working lives and receiving full benefits in their retirement years. They will also be different, however, in the growing economy that I assume will prevail in the long run after equilibrium is attained fifty years hence.

Investing in Treasury obligations would immediately, in 1998, change the budget balance by $87 billion, or 1 percent of projected GDP. This is the sum of the contributions of $104 billion minus the forgone income taxes of $21 billion, plus the interest saving to the Treasury of $4 billion on the average amount of reduced borrowing from the public, calculated at a 6.5 percent long-term rate of interest. In equilibrium, beginning in 2047, the contribution to surplus or to reduction in the deficit will be 1.96 percent of GDP, as shown in Table 6.1 (page 38). These figures compare with 1.39 percent of GDP and 0.76 percent for investment returns in the securities markets that were, respectively, 8 percent and 6.5 percent.

6

More and Less Optimistic Scenarios

If returns from investing in the stock market are at the optimistic rates (greater than 8 percent) suggested by many advocates of privatization, the benefits from supplementary contributions so invested will be greater. If the contrary occurs, they will be less. Table 6.1 (see page 38) offers some comparisons of long-run equilibrium results. With a 10 percent return on 3.1 percent of taxable payroll invested, there could be a positive contribution of 2.59 percent of GDP to the budget[1]—increasing the surplus and/or reducing the deficit by that amount—4.01 percent of GDP to additional benefits, and 61.9 percent of GDP to trust fund balances or net assets.

Results will be influenced, generally to a minor extent, by changes in the assumptions regarding trends in wage rates, prices, and cohort size. Aggregate results, although not individual benefits, will be affected by applying the OASDI projections of future declines in the growth of cohort size and hence of aggregate contributions. This is illustrated in Table 6.2 (see page 39 and Appendix Table A2, from which Table 6.2 is abstracted), based on an 8 percent return from stock index funds, and in Table 6.3 (see page 40). In particular, slower growth in cohort size will bring less rapid expansion of taxable payrolls and GDP. The benefits-to-GDP ratio is therefore higher in 2047, the equilibrium year shown in Table 6.3. And that ratio rises slightly afterward as the retirees-to-contributors and benefits-to-contributions ratios continue to rise. This would foretell a small decline in the contribution of the supplementary program to budget surplus. The ratio of fund assets to GDP is somewhat higher as contributions from early, more rapidly growing cohorts are matched with a less quickly expanding GDP.[2]

The measured budget surplus or deficit as a percentage of GDP is only trivially affected by alterations in the assumed rates of price inflation and wage increases. Increasing the rate of return credited to fund balances, however, increases benefits and fund

Table 6.1. Effects of Investing Supplementary Contributions on Budget Balance, Benefits, and Fund Assets at Equilibrium*

Investment	Rate of Return	Contribution toward Budget Surplus**	Benefits	Fund Assets
		(% of GDP)		
Indexed Funds	10.0	2.59	4.01	61.9
Indexed Funds	8.0	1.39	2.47	46.1
Indexed Funds	6.5	0.76	1.72	37.4
Indexed Funds	6.0	0.59	1.53	35.0
Indexed Funds	5.0	0.30	1.20	30.8
Treasuries	6.5	1.96	1.72	37.4
Treasuries	6.0	1.80	1.53	35.0
Treasuries	5.5	1.64	1.36	32.8

* Investing 3.1 percent of taxable payroll in indexed funds and in Treasury securities with various rates of return; cohort size grows at 1 percent per year so that aggregate contributions grow at 5 percent per year.

** This will depend on portion of return in cash or converted to cash by Treasury and then "borrowed" from trust funds.

Source: Author's calculations based on indicated assumptions.

asset ratios as well as the contribution (to the extent that it is in cash) to the budgetary position.

Aggregate results will be affected by participants' choices of investments. The long historical record of greater returns from equity (stock) than from fixed-income obligations (bonds) reflects in considerable part perceived differences in risk. Given the general aversion to risk, perhaps a disproportionate aversion to risk of loss, investors in the stock market need the inducement of greater total returns, in capital gains and dividends, than they can expect from bonds. Many participants, though, may want their supplementary pensions, as well as their basic Social Security benefits, to be more secure. They may opt in considerable part, if not in whole, for the relative safety of corporate

Table 6.2. Benefits as Percentage of Contributions, with 8 Percent Return, and Effects on Budgetary Position, Benefits, and Fund Assets as Percentages of GDP*

Year	Benefits (% of contributions)	Contribution toward Budget Surplus** (% of GDP)	Benefits (% of GDP)	Fund Assets (% of GDP)
2007	11.4	0.69	0.14	14.0
2017	54.8	1.52	0.66	29.9
2027	137.9	1.81	1.66	43.7
2037	220.9	1.55	2.66	50.2
2047	251.5	1.36	3.03	51.3
2057	253.2	1.37	3.05	51.6
2070	258.4	1.35	3.11	52.0
2075	260.4	1.34	3.14	52.2

* At ten-year intervals and extrapolated to 2070 and 2075; size of cohorts increasing for successive ten-year periods at rates of 1.01, 1.02, 0.43, -0.04, 0.29, 0.23, 0.02, 0.13, and 0.12 percent.

** If all of return is in cash or converted to cash.

Source: Author's calculations based on indicated assumptions.

Table 6.3. Supplementary Benefits in 2047 as Percentage of Contributions and Effects on Budgetary Position, Benefits, and Fund Assets as Percentages of GDP*

W/P	P	r	Benefits (percentage of contributions)	Contribution toward Budget Surplus** (percentage of GDP)	Benefits (percentage of GDP)	Fund Assets (percentage of GDP)
(percent per annum)						
0.9	2.1	8.0	321.8	1.38	3.91	60.37
0.9	2.5	8.0	290.1	1.39	3.52	56.50
1.425	2.5	8.0	251.5	1.36	3.03	51.30
0.9	3.5	8.0	224.8	1.37	2.70	48.15
0.9	3.5	9.054	288.6	2.03	3.46	56.99

* With real wage growth, *W/P*, of 0.9 percent per annum; price inflation, *P*, of 2.1, 2.5, and 3.5 percent; and rate of return, *r*, of 8.0 percent with price inflation of 3.5 percent.

** If all return is in cash or converted to cash.

Source: Author's calculations based on indicated assumptions.

bonds or the virtually complete guarantee of Treasury securities, even at the considerable sacrifice of expected income.

Simulations by the Social Security Administration itself, applying my proposal to their database and projections, would certainly differ in detail. They cannot be expected, however, to show significant departures from the results presented here.

7

Conclusion

So there is my proposal in all its simplicity. It preserves Social Security as we know it, increases—instead of cutting—retirement income for most Americans, helps keep the trust funds solvent, significantly reduces any budget deficits, and encourages more personal saving. All on a voluntary basis, with no increase in taxes!

Americans can have all of the benefits the would-be privatizers of Social Security claim with none of the major drawbacks of privatization. Administrative costs would be minimal, as all of the supplementary contributions, balances, and benefits would be blended with the accounts already in the Social Security computers. The stock and bond funds in which Social Security would invest would carry virtually no additional expenses. These funds would receive one large check each month for the total amount that all covered workers contribute and would merely have to report back to Social Security the value of and income on the total amount invested. Millions of Americans with little or no experience in investment would be spared the complexities of the financial world. The ever present risks of stock market fluctuations would be effectively insulated from the basic social insurance of our current system, which has kept so many elderly out of poverty.

Cutting the retirement benefits or other "entitlements" that a rich and great economy has been able to provide has no part in my picture. Our Social Security system ain't broke. There is no excuse for emasculating it in the guise of fixing it. And there is certainly no justification for socking the elderly. They should be helped. Old age is hard enough.

Appendixes

A1. Calculations for Constant Rate of Growth in Size of Cohorts

A2. Calculations for Lower Future Rate of Growth of Cohort Size

Table A1. Calculations for Constant Rate of Growth in Size of Cohorts

Year	Contributions $ Billions	End-of-Year Fund Balance $ Billions	Income Taxes $ Billions	Investing in Index		GDP $ Billions	Benefits Paid % of GDP	Fund Balance % of GDP	OASDI Int. Projection Balance* $ Billions
				Budget Surplus $ Billions	Budget Surplus % of GDP				
1998	103.9	108.0	-20.8	-16.4	-0.190567	8,632.1	0.0000	1.251	729
1999	109.0	229.8	-21.8	-8.5	-0.093776	9,063.7	0.0028	2.535	815
2000	114.5	366.4	-22.7	0.3	0.003231	9,516.8	0.0084	3.850	907
2001	120.2	519.0	-23.7	10.0	0.100256	9,992.7	0.0169	5.194	1,005
2002	126.2	688.7	-24.7	20.7	0.197091	10,492.3	0.0284	6.564	1,109
2003	132.5	876.7	-25.6	32.3	0.293516	11,016.9	0.0428	7.958	1,219
2004	139.2	1,084.4	-26.4	45.0	0.389297	11,567.8	0.0603	9.374	1,335
2005	146.1	1,312.9	-27.3	58.8	0.484191	12,146.2	0.0808	10.809	1,459
2006	153.4	1,563.6	-28.0	73.7	0.577938	12,753.5	0.1045	12.260	1,588
2007	161.1	1,837.9	-28.7	89.8	0.670264	13,391.1	0.1315	13.725	1,723
2008	169.2	2,137.2	-29.3	107.0	0.760882	14,060.7	0.1617	15.200	1,862
2009	177.6	2,463.0	-29.8	125.4	0.849488	14,763.7	0.1953	16.682	2,002
2010	186.5	2,816.5	-30.1	145.1	0.935762	15,501.9	0.2324	18.169	2,141
2011	195.8	3,199.3	-30.3	165.9	1.019365	16,277.0	0.2730	19.655	2,277
2012	205.6	3,612.7	-30.3	188.0	1.099942	17,090.9	0.3172	21.138	2,408
2013	215.9	4,058.1	-30.1	211.2	1.177117	17,945.4	0.3651	22.613	2,531
2014	226.7	4,536.8	-29.6	235.6	1.250495	18,842.7	0.4168	24.077	2,642
2015	238.0	5,050.1	-28.9	261.1	1.319661	19,784.8	0.4724	25.525	2,738
2016	249.9	5,599.1	-27.9	287.5	1.384175	20,774.1	0.5321	26.952	2,815
2017	262.4	6,184.7	-26.5	314.9	1.443576	21,812.8	0.5959	28.354	2,868
2018	275.5	6,807.9	-24.7	343.0	1.497378	22,903.4	0.6639	29.725	2,892

(cont. on the following page)

Table A1. Calculations for Constant Rate of Growth in Size of Cohorts (cont.)

				Investing in Index						
Year	Contributions $Billions	End-of-Year Fund Balance $Billions	Income Taxes $Billions	Budget Surplus $Billions	Budget Surplus % of GDP	GDP $Billions	Benefits Paid % of GDP	Fund Balance % of GDP	OASDI Int. Projection Balance* $Billions
2019	289.3	7,469.7	-22.5	371.9	1.546523	24,048.6	0.7346	31.061	2,882
2020	303.8	8,171.1	-20.0	401.7	1.590636	25,251.0	0.8080	32.359	2,834
2021	319.0	8,912.7	-16.9	432.0	1.629323	26,513.5	0.8843	33.615	2,742
2022	334.9	9,695.0	-13.3	462.7	1.662170	27,839.2	0.9635	34.825	2,607
2023	351.7	10,518.4	-9.2	493.6	1.688741	29,231.2	1.0458	35.984	2,421
2024	369.3	11,382.8	-4.4	524.4	1.708575	30,692.7	1.1313	37.086	2,175
2025	387.7	12,287.7	1.1	554.7	1.721188	32,227.4	1.2202	38.128	1,866
2026	407.1	13,232.2	7.4	584.1	1.726072	33,838.8	1.3125	39.104	1,486
2027	427.5	14,215.0	14.6	612.1	1.722691	35,530.7	1.4083	40.008	1,033
2028	448.8	15,233.9	22.7	638.1	1.710484	37,307.2	1.5079	40.834	501
2029	471.3	16,289.8	31.3	664.5	1.696236	39,172.6	1.6026	41.585	-112
2030	494.8	17,383.7	40.3	691.1	1.680161	41,131.2	1.6925	42.264	-812
2031	519.6	18,516.4	49.6	718.0	1.662479	43,187.8	1.7774	42.874	-1,606
2032	545.6	19,689.1	59.4	745.2	1.643419	45,347.2	1.8575	43.419	-2,500
2033	572.8	20,902.9	69.5	772.9	1.623221	47,614.5	1.9328	43.900	-3,499
2034	601.5	22,159.1	80.0	801.0	1.602134	49,995.2	2.0032	44.322	-4,607
2035	631.6	23,459.2	90.9	829.6	1.580419	52,495.0	2.0687	44.688	-5,829
2036	663.1	24,804.9	102.1	859.0	1.558348	55,119.8	2.1294	45.002	-7,173
2037	696.3	26,198.1	113.7	889.1	1.536204	57,875.7	2.1852	45.266	-8,645
2038	731.1	27,641,1	125.6	920.2	1.514285	60,769.5	2.2362	45.485	-10,252
2039	767.7	29,136.3	137.7	952.6	1.492899	63,808.0	2.2822	45.662	-12,003
2040	806.0	30,686.6	150.1	986.5	1.472373	66,998.4	2.3233	45.802	-13,909

Year	Contributions $Billions	End-of-Year Fund Balance $Billions	Income Taxes $Billions	Investing in Index: Budget Surplus $Billions	Investing in Index: Budget Surplus % of GDP	GDP $Billions	Benefits Paid % of GDP	Fund Balance % of GDP	OASDI Int. Projection Balance* $Billions
2041	846.3	32,295.6	162.7	1,022.2	1.453045	70,348.3	2.3594	45.908	-15,983
2042	888.7	33,967.1	175.4	1,060.2	1.435270	73,865.7	2.3905	45.985	-18,240
2043	933.1	35,705.6	188.2	1,100.9	1.419421	77,559.0	2.4165	46.037	-20,696
2044	979.7	37,516.6	201.1	1,144.9	1.405886	81,437.0	2.4375	46.068	-23,368
2045	1,028.7	39,406.1	213.8	1,192.9	1.395074	85,508.8	2.4533	46.084	-26,275
2046	1,080.2	41,381.2	226.4	1,245.7	1.387411	89,784.3	2.4639	46.084	-29,434
2047	1,134.2	43,450.3	238.7	1,304.1	1.383346	94,273.5	2.4693	46.090	-32,870
2048	1,190.9	45,622.8	250.7	1,369.3	1.383346	98,987.2	2.4693	46.090	36,605
2049	1,250.4	47,903.9	263.2	1,437.8	1.383346	103,936.5	2.4693	46.090	-40,664
2050	1,313.0	50,299.1	276.4	1,509.7	1.383346	109,133.4	2.4693	46.090	-45,075
2051	1,378.6	52,814.1	290.2	1,585.2	1.383346	114,590.0	2.4693	46.090	-49,871
2052	1,447.5	55,454.8	304.7	1,664.4	1.383346	120,319.5	2.4693	46.090	-55,086
2053	1,519.9	58,227.5	319.9	1,747.7	1.383346	126,335.5	2.4693	46.090	-60,754
2054	1,595.9	61,138.9	335.9	1,835.0	1.383346	132,652.3	2.4693	46.090	-66,913
2055	1,675.7	64,195.8	352.7	1,926.8	1.383346	139,284.9	2.4693	46.090	-73,602
2056	1,759.5	67,405.6	370.4	2,0231	1.383346	146,249.1	2.4693	46.090	-80,860
2057	1,847.5	70,775.9	388.9	2,124.3	1.383346	153,561.6	2.4693	46.090	-88,733
2058	1,939.8	74,314.7	408.3	2,230.5	1.383346	161,239.7	2.4693	46.090	-97,262
2070	3,483.7	133,458.6	733.3	4,005.7	1.383346	289,563.3	2.4693	46.090	-272,035
2075	4,446.1	170,330.7	935.9	5,112.4	1.383346	369,564.3	2.4693	46.090	-405,321

* Projections provided by the Office of the Actuary of the Social Security Administration.

Note: Contributions, c, of $706.46 in 1998 by members of each cohort aged 35 to 64, increasing for up to n years at rate of nominal wage growth, w; rate of return, r, credited each year to average fund balances; retirement benefits paid for m years; benefits scaled down by k to accommodate COLA of p; size of chohorts increasing at g per year; c = 3.1% of taxable payroll, $n = 30$, $w = 3.96\%$, $r = 8\%$, $k = 0.8007382749$, $p = 2.5\%$, $g = 1\%$. Budget surplus results assume all of return is in cash or converted to cash.

Table A2. Calculations for Lower Future Rate of Growth of Cohort Size

Year	Supp. Contri-butions $ Billions	Supp. Fund Balance $ Billions	OASDI Intermed. Projection of Balance $ Billions	Supp. Benefits Paid $ Billions	Supp. Benefits Paid % of Contrib.	Supp. Income Taxes $ Billions	Income from Supp. Average Balance $ Billions	Supp. Budget Surplus $ Billions	Supp. Budget Surplus % of GDP	Fund Balance Ratio of Supp. Benefits	Supp. Benefits Paid % of GDP	Supp. Fund Balance % of GDP
1998	104	108	729	0	0.00	-21	4	-16	-0.19	—	0.00	1.25
1999	109	230	815	0	0.23	-22	14	-8	-0.09	899.61	0.00	2.54
2000	114	366	907	1	0.71	-23	24	0	0.00	452.59	0.01	3.87
2001	119	517	1,005	2	1.43	-24	35	10	0.10	303.30	0.02	5.22
2002	125	686	1,109	3	2.40	-24	48	21	0.20	228.44	0.03	6.61
2003	131	871	1,219	5	3.63	-25	62	32	0.30	183.35	0.04	8.03
2004	137	1,076	1,335	7	5.14	-26	78	45	0.40	153.14	0.06	9.48
2005	143	1,301	1,459	10	6.92	-27	95	59	0.49	131.43	0.08	10.96
2006	150	1,546	1,588	13	8.99	-27	114	73	0.59	115.04	0.11	12.46
2007	156	1,814	1,723	18	11.36	-28	134	89	0.69	102.19	0.14	13.99
2008	163	2,105	1,862	23	14.05	-28	157	106	0.78	91.81	0.17	15.54
2009	170	2,421	2,002	29	17.06	-28	181	124	0.87	83.23	0.21	17.12
2010	178	2,762	2,141	36	20.41	-28	207	143	0.97	76.01	0.25	18.70
2011	186	3,129	2,277	45	24.12	-28	236	163	1.06	69.82	0.29	20.30
2012	194	3,524	2,408	55	28.20	-28	266	184	1.14	64.45	0.34	21.91
2013	202	3,948	2,531	66	32.67	-27	299	206	1.22	59.72	0.39	23.52
2014	211	4,401	2,642	79	37.55	-26	334	228	1.30	55.53	0.45	25.14
2015	220	4,883	2,739	94	42.86	-25	371	252	1.38	51.77	0.52	26.75
2016	229	5,397	2,815	112	48.62	-24	411	276	1.45	48.37	0.59	28.35
2017	239	5,941	2,869	131	54.84	-22	454	301	1.52	45.28	0.66	29.94
2018	249	6,516	2,892	154	61.57	-19	498	326	1.57	42.45	0.74	31.50

Year	Supp. Contri-butions $ Billions	Supp. Fund Balance $ Billions	OASDI Intermed. Projection of Balance $ Billions	Supp. Benefits Paid $ Billions	Supp. Benefits Paid % of Contrib.	Supp. Income Taxes $ Billions	Income from Supp. Average Balance $ Billions	Supp. Budget Surplus $ Billions	Supp. Budget Surplus % of GDP	Fund Balance Ratio of Supp. Benefits	Supp. Benefits Paid % of GDP	Supp. Fund Balance % of GDP
2019	260	7,122	2,882	178	68.66	-16	545	351	1.63	39.93	0.83	33.05
2020	271	7,759	2,834	206	76.07	-13	595	376	1.68	37.69	0.92	34.56
2021	282	8,427	2,742	236	83.80	-9	647	402	1.72	35.66	1.01	36.03
2022	294	9,126	2,607	270	91.89	-5	702	427	1.75	33.81	1.11	37.45
2023	306	9,855	2,421	307	100.33	0	759	452	1.78	32.10	1.21	38.82
2024	319	10,613	2,175	348	109.14	6	819	477	1.80	30.51	1.32	40.14
2025	332	11,399	1,866	393	118.33	12	880	500	1.81	29.02	1.43	41.39
2026	346	12,210	1,486	442	127.93	19	944	521	1.82	27.60	1.54	42.57
2027	360	13,045	1,033	497	137.94	27	1,010	541	1.81	26.26	1.66	43.67
2028	375	13,900	501	556	148.39	36	1,078	558	1.79	24.98	1.79	44.68
2029	390	14,775	-112	619	158.44	46	1,147	574	1.77	23.88	1.91	45.61
2030	407	15,669	-812	683	168.02	55	1,218	590	1.75	22.93	2.03	46.45
2035	498	20,437	-5,829	1,038	208.44	108	1,595	665	1.61	19.69	2.51	49.47
2036	519	21,452	-7,173	1,115	214.96	119	1,676	680	1.58	19.24	2.59	49.86
2037	540	22,489	-8,645	1,193	220.94	131	1,758	695	1.55	18.84	2.66	50.19
2038	563	23,548	-10,252	1,273	226.35	142	1,841	710	1.52	18.49	2.73	50.46
2039	586	24,633	-12,003	1,354	231.19	154	1,927	726	1.49	18.19	2.79	50.68
2040	610	25,744	-13,909	1,437	235.55	165	2,015	743	1.47	17.91	2.84	50.86
2041	635	26,882	-15,983	1,521	239.40	177	2,105	761	1.44	17.67	2.89	51.00
2042	662	28,050	-18,241	1,606	242.75	189	2,197	780	1.42	17.46	2.93	51.11
2043	689	29,251	-20,697	1,692	245.58	201	2,292	801	1.40	17.29	2.96	51.18
2044	717	30,488	-23,369	1,778	247.88	212	2,390	824	1.38	17.15	2.99	51.23
2045	747	31,765	-26,275	1,864	249.63	224	2,490	849	1.37	17.04	3.01	51.27
2046	778	33,086	-29,434	1,950	250.83	235	2,0594	878	1.36	16.97	3.02	51.30

(cont. on the following page)

Table A2. Calculations for Lower Future Rate of Growth of Cohort Size (concl.)

Year	Supp. Contri-butions $ Billions	Supp. Fund Balance $ Billions	OASDI Intermed. Projection of Balance $ Billions	Supp. Benefits Paid $ Billions	Supp. Benefits Paid % of Contrib.	Supp. Income Taxes $ Billions	Income from Supp. Average Balance $ Billions	Supp. Budget Surplus $ Billions	Supp. Budget Surplus % of GDP	Fund Balance Ratio of Supp. Benefits	Supp. Benefits Paid % of GDP	Supp. Fund Balance % of GDP
2047	809	34,458	-32,870	2,035	251.45	245	2,702	912	1.36	16.93	3.03	51.32
2048	843	35,888	-36,605	2,119	251.48	255	2,814	950	1.36	16.94	3.03	51.34
2049	877	37,376	-40,664	2,206	251.51	266	2,931	990	1.36	16.94	3.03	51.37
2050	913	38,927	-45,075	2,297	251.59	277	3,052	1,032	1.36	16.95	3.03	51.40
2051	950	40,542	-49,871	2,392	251.70	288	3,179	1,075	1.36	16.95	3.03	51.43
2052	989	42,224	-55,086	2,491	251.86	300	3,311	1,120	1.37	16.95	3.04	51.46
2053	1,029	43,974	-60,755	2,595	252.06	313	3,448	1,166	1.37	16.95	3.04	51.50
2054	1,071	45,795	-66,913	2,703	252.30	326	3,591	1,214	1.37	16.94	3.04	51.53
2055	1,115	47,689	-73,602	2,816	252.57	340	3,739	1,264	1.37	16.94	3.04	51.56
2056	1,160	49,660	-80,861	2,934	252.89	355	3,894	1,315	1.37	16.93	3.05	51.60
2057	1,207	51,708	-88,733	3,057	253.24	370	4,055	1,367	1.37	16.91	3.05	51.63
2058	1,256	53,838	-97,262	3,186	253.63	386	4,222	1,421	1.36	16.90	3.06	51.66
2070	2,025	87,377	-272,035	5,232	258.38	642	6,855	2,265	1.35	16.70	3.11	52.02
2075	2,470	106,912	-405,321	6,432	260.39	793	8,389	2,751	1.34	16.62	3.14	52.17

Note: Contributions, c, of $706.46 in 1998 by members of each cohort aged 35 to 64, increasing for up to n years at rate of nominal wage growth, w; rate of return, r, credited each year to average fund balances; retirement benefits paid for m years; benefits scaled down by k to accommodate COLA of p; size of cohorts increasing at g (cohort) per year—growth per annum for successive ten-year periods: 1.01%, 1.02%, 0.43%, -0.04%, 0.29%, 0.23%, 0.02%, 0.13%, and 0.12%; $c = 3.1\%$ of taxable payroll, $n = 30$, $w = 3.96\%$, $r = 8\%$, $k = 0.8007382749$, $p = 2.5\%$; investment in indexed stock or bond fund. Budget surplus results assume all of return is in cash or converted to cash. The assumed ten-year growth rates for cohorts are based on the intermediate alternative projections of total population aged 20 to 64 in the Social Security area, published in *Social Security Area Population Projections: 1997*, Actuarial Study No. 112, Social Security Administration, Office of the Chief Actuary, August 1997, SSA Pub: No. 11-11553, Table 21, pp. 84, 86, 88, 90, 92, 94, 96, 98 and 99.

Notes

2

1. *1997 Annual Report of the Board of Trustees of the Federal Old-Age and Survivors Insurance and Disability Insurance Trust Funds*, Washington, D.C., transmitted April 24, 1997, hereafter referred to as *OASDI Report*, p. 4, and Social Security Administration news release of October 16, 1997.

2. *Report of the 1994–1996 Advisory Council on Social Security*, vol. 1, hereafter referred to as *Advisory Council Report*, p. 89.

3. Total retirement benefits received in 1994 were $584.3 billion, of which 47.8 percent came from Social Security and 52.2 percent from the sum of private pensions (30.7 percent), Federal Employee Retirement programs (11.0 percent), and State and Local Employee Retirement programs (10.5 percent) as indicated in *EBRI Databook on Employee Benefits*, 4th ed. (Washington, D.C.: Employee Benefit Research Institute, 1997), p. 155 (hereafter referred to as *EBRI Databook*).

4. The Monthly Benefit Data Base maintained by the Office of the Chief Actuary of the Social Security Administration put the average monthly figure for 1996 at $792.66.

5. *Social Security Reform* (New York: Twentieth Century Fund Press, 1996).

6. *Advisory Council Report*, p. 19.

3

1. By way of explanation, see Robert Eisner, "Don't Sock the Elderly, Help Them: Old Age Is Hard Enough," *Elder Law Journal* (University of Illinois) 5, no. 1 (Spring 1997): 181–93; Robert Eisner,

The Great Deficit Scares: The Federal Budget, Trade, and Social Security (New York: Twentieth Century Fund Press, 1997).

2. *The Economic and Budget Outlook: Fiscal Years 1997–2006*, Congressional Budget Office, May 1996, pp. xix and xxi.

3. *The Economic and Budget Outlook: Fiscal Years 1998–2007*, Congressional Budget Office, January 1997, p. xviii.

4. See *OASDI Report*, p. 60.

5. "The Economic and Budget Outlook for Fiscal Years 1999–2008: A Preliminary Report," Congressional Budget Office, January 7, 1998, p. 2, www.cbo.gov.

6. *Advisory Council Report*, p. 89.

7. See Robert Eisner, "Whatever You Call It, a Tax Goes to the Treasury," *Wall Street Journal*, July 29, 1997.

8. *OASDI Report*, p. 53.

9. *EBRI Databook*, p. 179.

10. Olivia S. Mitchell, James M. Poterba, and Mark J. Warshawsky, "New Evidence on the Money's Worth of Individual Annuities," NBER Working Paper no. 6002, National Bureau of Economic Research, Cambridge, Mass., April 1997, p. 2.

11. *OASDI Report*, Table II.H1, p. 148.

12. Calculated as 100 x (1 - 1/1.0498) = 4.74 percent.

13. In response to concerns about Social Security, real and imagined,there has been a substantial agitation for "reform." I would reform Social Security to adjust some of the benefits and taxes in the direction of greater equity and efficiency. The payroll tax is focused particularly on labor, has no progressivity whatsoever, and had an upper income cut off point, $65,400 in 1997, rising to $68,400 in 1998. With use of a dedicated portion of the income tax Social Security might then offer benefits to all who contribute, including those whose income taxes have been based on capital income rather than labor income. There is no reason why all should not receive retirement insurance regardless of the sources of their income and contributions. The couple that lives off interest and dividends and capital gains, as well as employees on salaries and wages, should have the opportunity to receive an actuarially fair retirement annuity with protection against the possibility of ravaging inflation.

14. The "best estimate of the size of the upward bias" in the CPI inflation rate according to the Senate Finance Committee's Advisory Commission to Study the Consumer Price Index ("The Boskin Commission"), *Toward a More Accurate Measure of the Cost of Living*, December 4, 1996, p. ii.

15. If one really wanted to encourage people to work longer, it would make sense rather to remove the penalty of the loss of Social Security

for each full year the employee is over age 55" (p.11). Among FERS employees, 83 percent contribute; among CSRS employees, without the matching contributions, 54 percent participate (letter to employees from executive director, Federal Retirement Thrift Investment Board, Washington, D.C., March 1997.)

State and local government employees are overwhelmingly in defined benefit plans, but it may be noted that as of 1995, 51 percent of state and local pension fund investments were in equity, 32 percent in bonds, and 13 percent in "other" holdings, including mortgages, real estate, and mutual funds. *EBRI Databook*, p. 137.

19. This might occur if the federal deficit is reduced by cutting grants-in-aid to states and localities, currently running at more than $200 billion per year, or by transferring federal programs to them.

20. It is worth pointing out that the desirability of increased national saving, as it is currently measured, is far from clear. It has long been said that Japan has had rapid growth and great economic success because it has had a high rate of saving, while the United States has suffered greatly from its allegedly low rate of saving. The relative states of the Japanese and American economies today certainly call that link into question.

6

1. This would be correct if, as indicated in the note to Table 6.1, all of the return were in cash or converted to cash by the Treasury. The effect on the budget surplus or deficit would depend not on the total rate of return but on the portion of the return in cash or converted to cash. If, for example, only half of the 10 percent return were in cash the reduction in the budget deficit (or increase in the surplus) would be that shown on the 5 percent rate of return line, or only 0.30 percent of GDP.

2. Table 6.2 is abstracted from Appendix Table A2. The assumed ten-year growth rates for cohorts are based on the intermediate alternative projections of total population aged twenty to sixty-four in the Social Security area, published in *Social Security Area Population Projections: 1997,* Actuarial Study no. 112, Office of the Chief Actuary, Social Security Administration, August 1997, Table 21, pp. 84, 86, 88, 90, 92, 94, 96, 98, and 99.

I note a possibility of adverse selection affecting years of retirement that may be balanced by favorable selection regarding cohort size.

Those who do not expect to live as long, statistically minorities and more generally the poor, may not be as likely to sacrifice current consumption for future retirement benefits. But the cohorts of those actually contributing may grow, along with their contributions, among people expecting to live longer than the average life span.

Index

Robert Ei[illegible] [illegible]western
Universi[illegible] [illegible]ic Association. H[illegible] [illegible]rts and
Sciences ar[illegible] [illegible]d exten-
sively in pr[illegible] [illegible]frequent
columns o[illegible] [illegible]*al, New*
York Time[illegible] [illegible]dia. His
previous b[illegible] [illegible]*Federal*
Budget, T[illegible] [illegible]*erstood*
Economy: [illegible] *Real Is*
the Federal [illegible]*counts.*